MAGNUUM COOKING

(FOOD IS HEALTH)

BY

SUSAN NAMUGGA

U.S.A

TABLE OF CONTENTS

Cooking is a Virtue, and I enjoy it as much as eating the food I make. We learn it from our parents/guardians for survival reasons. Being the last born of five gave me lots of time to practice my taste in food. I am a picky eater to T- and making my own food became such a sport!

Above: My version of Tilapia Sandwich with tomatoes(A type of fish caught from fresh waters in East Africa) It was pan-seared, seasoned with salt, curry, and a little cayenne to taste. It is ready in 30minutes on high and low alternative.

Procedure:

- Wash, scale and clean the fish(tilapia)
- Drain all water.
- Slice the fish from the spine (Fillet fish)
- Turn the frying pan on heat.
- Add a little oil, not too much.
- Place the sliced fish into the pan, skin down.
- Season your fish.
- Sear to liking.
- Cover the pan and turn heat on low.
- Feel free to turn fish onto the other side for proper cooking.
- Let the fillet cool down and serve afterwards.
- Enjoy!!

Spaghetti party…

So many times, we dismiss cooking ideas, and our instinct on food. However, I try to embrace all ideas that pop-up in my head to make tasty foods.

Food is a sensation to all taste buds; While I grew on a simple meal plan, I choose to always spice it up!

My infamous Pan-Fried Pork.

Ingredients:

- A good piece of pork (with some fat)
- Onions, garlic, spices
- Curry Powder
- Salt

- Pepper
- Tomatoes
- Cabbages (if you like them)
- Frying Pan
- Some oil if meat is not fatty.

Preparation.

- Wash your piece of chosen meat (pork in this case)
- Cut it into cubes or similar.
- Put the pork into a pan.
- Put the frying pan onto a stove and turn it on
- Add oil if needed.
- Cover the frying pan with meat/pork.
- As it heats up and seers, check on it and turn it around the pan.
- Let it cook until water is almost dry.
- Pork turns brownish and is mostly cooked.
- Chop, dice and prepare the ingredients as needed.
- Put garlic first to eliminate meat scent and add the rest accordingly.
- Add curry powder, salt, and pepper last.
- Cover the pan after each step.
- Voila` pork is ready in under an hour.
- Bon Appetit`

Home mad PiZZA....is a Love Language!!!

Honestly, I winged this one! I had the flour, and potatoes with several hand skills. I decided to whip it. I came out great! With baking flour, I think that was ketch up, leftover meat and sliced potatoes.

STEPS:

- Put flour in a bowl as needed.
- Add some baking powder/yeast for the dough to rise.
- Add salt.
- Add some oil.
- Add some water, lukewarm.
- Mix everything together.
- Knead your dough until medium hardened.
- Cover your dough for 10minutes.
- Pre-Heat Oven At 350-400 degrees
- Roll the dough into a circular shape.
- Place the flat dough onto a baking tray.
- Add ingredients for pizza.
- Tomato sauce, onions, beef or pepperoni, Cheese as needed.
- Cook for 20 t0 25 minutes in Oven on high.
- Switch to broil for the top part to prep.
- Slice and serve when ready!

The idea of Cuisines seems far-fetched to fit the African taste, and yet most African food is all Natural and easy to digest! I always eat some of that to feel the taste of home! On Sundays, my mom cooks or I do; And when I do, it serves the purpose!

You might be wondering, what African food? I am Originally from Uganda, and Matooke/green bananas are our staple in the Central region. We make it with banana leaves and cook some beef with it. Sometimes, other proteins show up. However, the main course is the center piece!

Ready bananas with fish…. Ugandan style

Banana with chicken soup

Banana, rice, and pork soup

This is bananas, rice with groundnuts sauce and some pork.

The fascination is in the taste, but preparation is fun too. Here is what we need.

Meal Preparation.

- Green bananas (from an Indian store)
- Beef or a protein
- Vegetables or other foods to add to the feast.

STEPS:

1. Peel and wash the green/cream bananas.
2. Boil them in a pan until soft.
3. Drain water and mash them.
4. Wrap them into banana leaves r foil paper.
5. Put them in the oven to keep them soft.

6. Prepare other foods and vegetables to serve with
7. Prepare beef stew/ protein.
8. For beef, smoke the beef in oven prior to prep day.
9. Add water in a pan with ingredients and salt.
10. Let it boil until ready.
11. Serve with bananas and other foods and vegetables as seen above.

Fast food in house looks surreal.

One time I decide to make a breakfast burger with fries/sweet potato fries. It turned out great.

I got buns from the store, cut up some sweet potato strings, and fried eggs. I heated up a frying pan, made some eggs, and deep fried the sweet potato fries. Put into my bun and rocked the boat. It was awesome with some ketch up!

Sweet potato wedges…. ready for preparation

All types of Sandwiches... delicacy yet? You bet... porklicious...

Balance is life…. Salad is good always! I love Ranch on it.

Besides all the food so far, I take these pictures using my phone because they are my memory of good food. It is paramount that everyone gets the best food out of life.

Pancakes are life and I make them from scratch! Put some bananas on top, voila` magic!

Process:

1. Pour some baking flour in a bowl.
2. Add some honey or sugar.
3. Add water or milk.
4. Stir until fine.
5. Heat up a frying pan.
6. Add oil or butter.
7. Pour mix into hot pan and observe for color change.
8. Turn pancake onto the other side and do the same.

9. Serve with fruit or honey/syrup.

My signature sweet potatoes...Sliced and fried... Tasty!!

Dinner is served! Chapati, beans and sweet potato Slices. YUM!

As seen above, Chapatiz are popular in East Africa, and we carry it with us to the diaspora. I make them and eat them all the time. They are an easier meal when hungry! They are like flatbread and yet the method of making them is different.

Single chapati about to be eaten!

These are Chapatiz ready to be served!

HOW TO MAKE CHAPATIZ?

Ingredients:

- Baking flour (Unbleached/King Arthur)
- Cooking oil (Olive oil is legit)
- Salt
- Onions (Red ones for me)
- Warm water
- Big bowl
- Cutting board
- Roller pin
- Frying pan/cast iron
- Fireplace/ stove
- Polythene bag/plastic bag (for keeping chapatiz soft)
- Paper Towel

1. STEPS.
2. Pour a good amount of baking flour (two cups)
3. Cut up some onions to your liking and add them into the flour.
4. Get a pinch of salt or two for taste.
5. Add a little oil in the flour.
6. Add warm water, and mix.
7. Use both hands to work the flour into a solid moist dough.
8. (The machine works as well; hands are the traditional method preferred)
9. When the dough is fine and ready,
10. Cover it up with a kitchen cloth for at least 10-15minutes.

11.   Pinch big balls of dough and make several of them.

12.   Oil one ball at a time working inwards. Then flatten it on the chopping board.

13.   Add some dry flour on

    a. the board and press the flat dough with the rolling pin until round and flat.

14.   Turn on the heat and place your frying pan on it. Put the flattened dough onto the heated pan, let it heat up and add a little oil on top.

15.   Flip the unready chapati and cook the other side.

16.   When it is brownish, take it off and put in a plastic bag with paper towel inside. 16.   Repeat Steps 11 to 15 until all dough balls are made flat and fried.

17.   Enjoy the taste of

    a. Africa!

CHAPATIZ

My go to breakfast, Oatmeal plus fruit and raisins

Besides my kitchen centeredness, I also eat out on Occasions, and when I do it is either Pizza from Bertucci or KFC. It feels like something that saves me from hobby, but I love to eat out as well.

Corn meal/Posho with beans, Brussel sprouts and vegetables
Ingredients.

1. Maize flour (for corn meal)
2. Boiled water
3. A pan
4. Mingling stick
5. Stove

Process:

- Boil water like 4 cups
- Put some corn flour in the pan.
- Add some hot water to the flour.
- Stir to mix.
- Put it on stove on moderate heat.
- Add more flour as much as you need.
- Add hot water and mingle.
- Until texture is consistent and non-sticky • Put it on a plate when you are done for aeration.
- Serve with sauce.

Grapes and watermelon snack

In fact, the only recommended sugar one can have is that of fruits. They help reboot the body right away especially when you are hungry. By eating fruit, you are Nourishing the body!

Beet root

Strawberry Milkshake

Pineapple and blue berries

Whichever food we choose to eat, it must contribute to our own wellbeing! Satisfaction is good, but fulfillment *is even better. It is paramount that we eat well within our means.*

Homemade fries, fried cassava and plantain, white beans

Choosing which type of meals to serve at your table varies from house to house, and yet the number of options is enormous. We can draw from other cultures always!

34

Plantain Strips, Fried eggs, and Tomatoes

Ingredients.

- Plantains

- Eggs
- Fresh tomatoes
- Frying pan
- Cooking oil
- Salt
- Frying pan

Process.

1. Peel your plantains.
2. Slice plantains longitudinally
3. Heat up a frying pan.
4. Put some oil in the pan.
5. Place the plantain one by one.
6. Turn both sides of plantain.
7. Place brown plantain on paper towel to drain oil.
8. Put some salt on the plantain.
9. Serve
10. Fry some eggs and slice tomatoes altogether and enjoy...

Sue's Chicken

Everyone fries Chicken!! But I fry chicken Legs also known as Drumsticks.

I am big on Flavor, I love Aroma! I love chicken... However, this was a masterpiece. Doing this gave me a lot of boosts to stay in the kitchen. STEPS;

- First wash your chicken
- Heat up some oil more than enough oil.
- Dry the chicken with paper towel.
- Dip it in oil at medium temperature.
- Take out chicken when it looks brown.
- Hang it on a rack.

- Let it cool down.
- Sieve oil and heat it up again.
- Re-fry the fried chicken
- Drain chicken and cut fresh red onions on top of them.
- SALT
- Serve

_Chicken with Salad

Fillet fish with rice and Avocado

Water Down

FRENCH TOAST IN BUTTER WITH EGGS AND TOMATOES

Steamed Maize/ Corn and ripened green bananas.

44

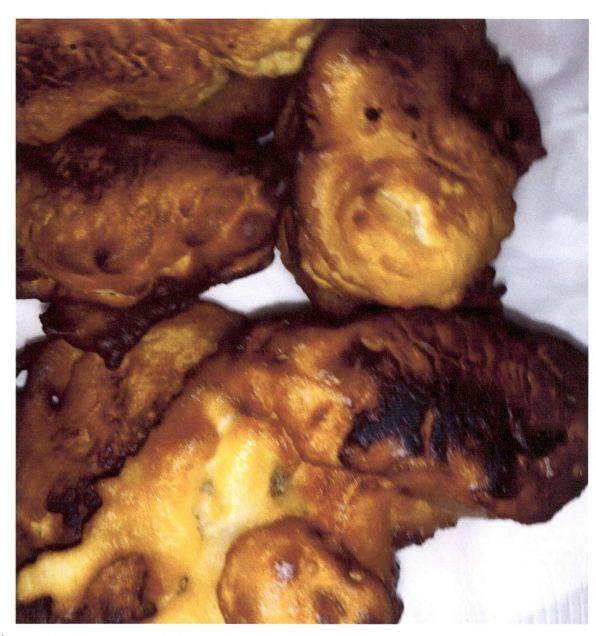

Beignets/ Mandashi in Kiswahili

Beignets are popular all over the world, especially in France and in East Africa. Making them is an interesting, sweet process.

Ingredients for beignets.

- Baking flour (Unbleached)
- Sugar

- Baking powder (if you have some)
- Water/ Light milk
- Bowl
- Spatula STEPS.

1. Pour flour in a bowl.
2. Add sugar.
3. Add baking powder. Less than a teaspoon.
4. Add water till the texture is consistent.
5. Mix with a spatula.
6. Heat up a pan.
7. Add cooking oil.
8. Scoop mixture with a spatula and drop it in the hot oil gently.
9. Fry till brown.
10. Let them rest on a rack and serve when cool.

Cassava/Yuca with beans (Delicacy in East Africa)

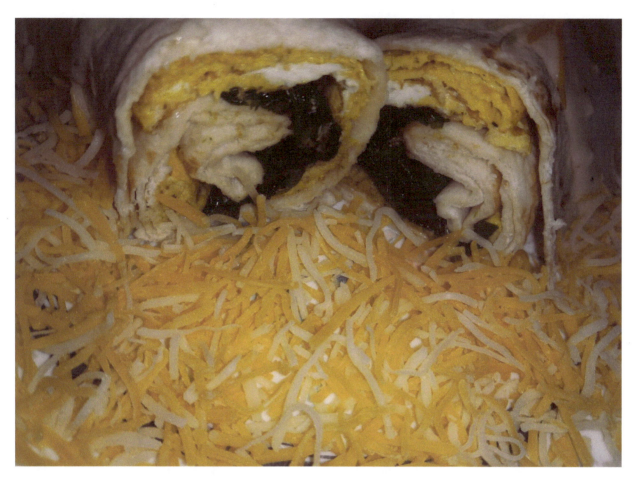

That cheese roll was awesome.

I felt like raw cheese tastes better. Roll some eggs with it, and veggies on a flat bread. This is awesome!! It is a great choice on a lazy cooking day.

Seasoned baked Tilapia (My signature dish) All I do is put salt, pepper, cayenne, garlic, and curry. I put some oil and place it in the Oven. The rest is yumminess!!

Lazy fish dish (Tilapia)

Pottage (A mixture of cassava with beans)

The one recipe for pottage (mix) is basically made by peeling cassava/yuca, cutting and washing the root crop. Prepare your beans, and mix them with the pieces of cassava, boil until ready. Add salt, curry, and some olive oil to your liking. It is so tasty you cannot even imagine!!

Salad in a pocket/flatbread pocket

The blunt food assortment; cassava, fried eggs, Brussel sprouts, plantain, tomatoes…..Yum!

While in the kitchen, the idea is to get the best out of it, and my best always comes down to being filled with healthy food. By trying to mix in various fruits and vegetables to achieve a rounded meal.

Pawpaw/Papaya

Papaya fruit

Strawberry bonanza (with milk) and bananas

Beignets served.

Rollex is a delicacy in E.A.

It is made with chapati as we saw prior, and fried eggs.

Whip up some eggs, fry them and put a chapati on top.

Flip it and add tomatoes and roll.

Cut it into slices and enjoy the bliss.

Rice balls

How to make rice balls_

Needs:

- Rice
- Baking flour
- Turmeric
- Cooking oil
- Salt
- water Steps.

1. Boil some rice.
2. Let the rice cool down.
3. Mix a little baking flour with water and turmeric
4. Heat up some cooking oil.
5. Make balls out of the rice.
6. Dip the balls into the flour mix.
7. Gently drop the balls in hot oil with a ladle.
8. Let them fry for a few seconds until firm and brownish.
9. Put them on a rack to drain oil.
10. Serve when cool.

Deep Fried yuca/Cassava

Sweet Potatoes and Irish potatoes ready for preparation

Fried potatoes, plantain, and bacon

These kinds of foods are good ideas for breakfast or lunch, and they make a great supplement to the fruits served as well as a warm cup of tea. This is anytime kind of food. It can be a craving too with the frying part. However, not to be eaten everyday but rather on occasions.

Samosas are an international treat; from India all the way to East Africa and the Middle East.

The fact that many cultures eat samosas is a clear distinction of this simple food. With only a few ingredients, we get the taste of culture. We usually fill them with peas and or minced meat. Samosas taste even better in person.

How to make Samosas.

Ingredients:

- Baking flour (to make baking sheets)
- Cooking oil
- A cup of water
- Salt
- Onions
- Peas/Minced meat
- Frying pan/Oven
- Curry
- Knife STEPS:

1. Make a dough, With water, flour, salt and oil.
2. Make single thin sheets from the dough.
3. Heat the sheets on the frying pan on both sides until brownish/marked.
4. Let the sheets cool off.
5. Cut the sheets/Flat thin bread into halves.
6. Prepare the peas by boiling/Prepare the minced meat for use.
7. Add diced onions, and curry to the peas/meat.
8. Make a thick consistency of flour, water and salt sealing the samosas.

9.   With both hands, roll the half sheets of flat bread into a cone-like shape, seal the side with our consistency of thick flour and water.

10.   Put a spoonful or less of peas in the corn shaped sheet.

11.   Close it with the consistency we made.

12.   Make as many as you need.

13.   Heat up cooking oil and fry/ bake in oven.

14.   Take them out when they turn brownish.

15.   On a rack for oil to drip or use paper towel to remove excess oil.

16.   Enjoy the International Snack.

SAMOSAS

Sweetness Overload; French toast, eggs and honey with bananas

With butter melting on a hot pan, place the bread center, pour your egg mix on Top of the bread, turn all sides for brown texture. Plate them, slice your banana and pour some honey and taste it!

_The best way to the heart is through food, and food we have shared with the world! Remember to feed your gut and to always stay health! Enjoy the food, as much you enjoy yourselves.

FOODIE DIARIES
Susan Namugga
SN.

CPSIA information can be obtained
at www.ICGtesting.com
Printed in the USA
LVHW072027150323
741693LV00031B/1110